THE BILL OF RIGHTS

THE BILL OF RIGHTS: DEFINING OUR FREEDOMS

BY RICH SMITH

SERIES CONSULTANT: SCOTT HARR, J.D. CRIMINAL JUSTICE
DEPARTMENT CHAIR, CONCORDIA UNIVERSITY ST. PAUL

VISIT US AT
WWW.ABDOPUBLISHING.COM

Published by ABDO Publishing Company, 8000 West 78th Street, Suite 310, Edina, MN 55439.

Printed in the United States.

Editor: John Hamilton
Graphic Design: Sue Hamilton
Cover Design: Neil Klinepier
Cover Illustration: Corbis
Interior Photos and Illustrations: p 1 Constitution & flag, iStockphoto; p 5 *The Scene at the Signing of the Constitution*, courtesy of the Architect of the Capitol, Washington, D.C.; p 7 young man waving U.S. flag, Corbis; p 9 The Bill of Rights, courtesy the National Archives; p 11 replicas of historical documents on a scale, iStockphoto; p 13 Alexander Hamilton, Corbis; pp 14-15 duel between Aaron Burr and Alexander Hamilton, Corbis; pp 16-17 caricature of fight between Griswold and Lyon, Corbis; p 19 Articles of Confederation, courtesy the National Archives; p 21 James Madison, Corbis; p 22 James Madison, Corbis; p 23 James Madison and Thomas Jefferson, Corbis; p 24 James Madison, Corbis; p 25 Virginia Declaration of Rights, Corbis; p 26 King John signs the Magna Carta, Corbis; p 27 Magna Carta 1297, courtesy the National Archives; p 29 candle and quill with reproduction of the Bill of Rights, Corbis.

Library of Congress Cataloging-in-Publication Data

Smith, Rich, 1954-
 The Bill of Rights : defining our freedoms / Rich Smith.
    p. cm. -- (The Bill of Rights)
 Includes index.
 ISBN 978-1-59928-913-7
 1. United States. Constitution. 1st-10th Amendments--History--Juvenile literature. 2. Civil rights--United States--History--Juvenile literature. I. Title.

KF4750.S65 2008
342.7308'5--dc22
                    2007014544

CONTENTS

FOREWORD

BY SCOTT HARR, J.D. CRIMINAL JUSTICE DEPARTMENT CHAIR, CONCORDIA UNIVERSITY ST. PAUL

There are three things everyone agrees on when it comes to constitutional law: First, its importance. Second, how little most of us know about it. And third, how scared we can get by even *thinking* about learning it. After all, don't you need to be a lawyer to figure out constitutional law?

No! That's the beauty of this Abdo Publishing *Bill of Rights* series. Mr. Rich Smith has captured the essence of America's most important documents, the very foundation of the most successful legal system in the world, in a way that makes the study of our Constitution not only understandable, but fun.

Fun learning about the Constitution? Absolutely!

Starting with the birth of our nation, this series builds in a reasonable format and results in a wonderfully thorough foundation of knowledge. It proves that constitutional law doesn't have to be so complicated that only a lawyer can figure it out. Most writing in this area incorrectly assumes that everything in the Constitution needs to be addressed at once. It doesn't, certainly not at this point in a student's learning.

I would equate it to learning to snowboard or skateboard. No one learns either skill by studying the metallurgy that goes into building the products, or meteorology to know how to predict the best weather for playing outside. But that's how traditional constitutional law is taught; learn it all right now. No wonder students fear it. Lawyers do too! Mr. Smith builds a foundation and lets the reader learn a step at a time with each concept building upon itself. In no time the reader will be proclaiming, "Now I get it!"

Finally, without a reason to learn something, knowledge becomes nothing more than an exercise in memorization, the least fun and most ineffective way to learn. Rich Smith provides examples throughout this series for the reader to directly relate to. Suddenly it all makes sense because it's understandable and applies to real life, which by the way is exactly what the Framers of the Constitution intended in the first place.

The fact is, the United States Constitution affects everything we do, every day of our lives. Because of the Constitution and the Bill of Rights, we are free to go where we want, do what we want, and see and listen to what we want (with some important exceptions). No other law sets America apart from other countries as does our Constitution. To this day its promise continues to motivate people to risk their lives to be able to live with the freedoms it guarantees.

I commend Rich Smith and Abdo Publishing for providing a meaningful, stimulating, and yes, fun way to learn about the Constitution. *You do have a right to learn this way!*

Above: A painting by Howard Chandler Christy entitled *The Scene at the Signing of the Constitution.* More than two centuries later, the United States Constitution continues to guarantee and protect the freedoms of all Americans.

NATURAL RIGHTS: BORN WITH FREEDOM

Just for fun, make a list of the things you own. Items that would probably be on your list include clothes, a bike, a skateboard, video games, DVDs, books, an MP3 player, and other cool stuff. Your list may be short or it may be long. The important thing is that all the items on your list belong to you. You own them. That means nobody is allowed to take them from you.

Now look over your list again. Is something missing? Very possibly you left off the most valuable items you own. And you probably left them off because they are things you don't think about much. What are they? Your freedoms.

In the United States of America, you own freedoms even though you didn't buy them. You didn't have to. You own them just because you are a human being. And you have owned them from the moment you were born.

The United States was started in 1776. But the idea that humans are born owning freedom started only about 100 years before then. It was quite a strange idea for its time. Freedom was something enjoyed by very few people throughout all of history. The only people who really could say they were born with freedom were kings and queens and emperors.

The idea that all people own freedom beginning at birth comes from a belief in what is known as *natural rights*. The theory about natural rights goes something like this: Humans do what they do because it's built into them, and what they crave most of all are life, liberty, and happiness.

Left: A boy waves a flag by the Lincoln Memorial. Since the United States was formed, one of the country's most important ideas was that all people were born with natural rights to certain freedoms.

Believers in natural rights take this basic idea one step further. They say that since humans naturally want life, liberty, and happiness, it would be unnatural to deny them those things. Therefore, humans have an automatic right to life, liberty, and the pursuit of happiness, the same as they have a right to breathe air. If this is true, then governments cannot forbid the people from enjoying such rights. The concept here is that government can't take away what it didn't give.

THE BILL OF RIGHTS

Theories about natural rights may sound nice. But how can you be sure that you actually own any freedoms today? You know it because a group of men known as the Founding Fathers of the United States made up an official list of freedoms called the Bill of Rights. "Rights" is a word that means "owned freedoms." Freedoms you own are rights that cannot be taken away by the government.

The Bill of Rights is found at the end of the Constitution of the United States. The Constitution is a document that describes how the U.S. government is set up and operated. It also explains the job of the president, the members of Congress, and the people who work as judges. Most importantly, the Constitution and the Bill of Rights tell the government it cannot stop the American people from fully using and enjoying the rights they were born with unless the government has a really, really good reason for doing so.

The Constitution has been around for a very long time. It was written in 1787, but it did not become the highest law of the land together with the Bill of Rights until 1791. Representatives of the people in each state carefully discussed what they liked and didn't like about the proposed Constitution. Then they took a vote. In 1791, the United States officially approved the Constitution combined with the Bill of Rights, creating a new kind of government that still exists to this day.

The freedoms of the people and the limits on government power that are listed at the end of the Constitution have grown since 1791. Today, there are 27 separately listed freedoms and limits on government power, each of which is called an amendment. The Bill of Rights is made up of the first 10 amendments.

Above: The Bill of Rights is currently housed in the National Archives building in Washington, D.C. It was mainly written by Founding Father James Madison. He took more than 200 suggested amendments from the states and chose the best among them to be in the Bill of Rights. Madison's original version had 12 amendments to the Constitution. The first two were not ratified by the necessary three-fourths of the states, which is how the Bill of Rights came to be 10 amendments. In 1791, the United States officially approved the Constitution combined with the Bill of Rights, creating a new kind of government that still exists to this day.

- **First Amendment:** "Congress shall make no law respecting an establishment of religion, or prohibiting the free exercise thereof; or abridging the freedom of speech, or of the press; or the right of the people peaceably to assemble, and to petition the Government for a redress of grievances."

- **Second Amendment:** "A well regulated Militia, being necessary to the security of a free State, the right of the people to keep and bear Arms, shall not be infringed."

- **Third Amendment:** "No Soldier shall, in time of peace be quartered in any house, without the consent of the Owner, nor in time of war, but in a manner to be prescribed by law."

- **Fourth Amendment:** "The right of the people to be secure in their persons, houses, papers, and effects, against unreasonable searches and seizures, shall not be violated, and no Warrants shall issue, but upon probable cause, supported by Oath or affirmation, and particularly describing the place to be searched, and the persons or things to be seized."

- **Fifth Amendment:** "No person shall be held to answer for a capital, or otherwise infamous crime, unless on a presentment or indictment of a Grand Jury, except in cases arising in the land or naval forces, or in the Militia, when in actual service in time of War or public danger; nor shall any person be subject for the same offense to be twice put in jeopardy of life or limb; nor shall be compelled in any criminal case to be a witness against himself, nor be deprived of life, liberty, or property, without due process of law; nor shall private property be taken for public use, without just compensation."

- **Sixth Amendment:** "In all criminal prosecutions, the accused shall enjoy the right to a speedy and public trial, by an impartial jury of the State and district wherein the crime shall have been committed, which district shall have been previously ascertained by law, and to be informed of the nature and cause of the accusation; to be confronted with the witnesses against him; to have compulsory process for obtaining witnesses in his favor, and to have the Assistance of Counsel for his defense."

• **Seventh Amendment:** "In Suits at common law, where the value in controversy shall exceed twenty dollars, the right of trial by jury shall be preserved, and no fact tried by a jury, shall be otherwise re-examined in any Court of the United States, than according to the rules of the common law."

• **Eighth Amendment:** "Excessive bail shall not be required, nor excessive fines imposed, nor cruel and unusual punishments inflicted."

• **Ninth Amendment:** "The enumeration in the Constitution, of certain rights, shall not be construed to deny or disparage others retained by the people."

• **Tenth Amendment:** "The powers not delegated to the United States by the Constitution, nor prohibited by it to the States, are reserved for the States respectively, or to the people."

Above: Copies of the United States Declaration of Independence, the Constitution, and the Bill of Rights.

How the Bill of Rights Was Created

The Bill of Rights officially became part of the highest law of the land on December 15, 1791. For that to happen, no fewer than 11 of the 14 states that existed at the time had to agree to it. Believe it or not, many of the Founding Fathers were at first against the idea of including a bill of rights in the Constitution. They worried that Congress and the courts would look at the list and decide those were all the rights the people could ever possibly need. In that case, there would be no reason to ever expand on the rights with new laws and court rulings. The system, these people worried, would be too inflexible to withstand the test of time.

A Founding Father who didn't like the idea of a bill of rights was Alexander Hamilton of New York. He wrote essays arguing against it. These and other essays from two other Founding Fathers became known as *The Federalist Papers*. There were 85 of these essays in total. They were written mainly to stir up excitement about having a federal constitution, but without a bill of rights attached to it. *Federalist Paper Number 84* was the one in which Hamilton most strongly blasted away at the argument for a bill of rights.

The Federalist Papers helped people make up their minds about what should or should not be included in the Constitution. Today, Supreme Court justices and many others still read *The Federalist Papers* when they try to understand what the Founding Fathers meant when they wrote certain parts of the Constitution. In fact, *The Federalist Papers* are used more than any other source for information about the original intentions of the Constitution's Framers.

Alexander Hamilton made some very strong arguments against having a bill of rights. His point was that such a list of owned freedoms was unnecessary. He believed the Constitution all by itself was enough to guarantee people the ability to freely enjoy their natural rights.

Still, there were many people who thought Hamilton and his fellow Federalists were dead wrong. Those who opposed Hamilton warned that it would be a horrible mistake for the Founding Fathers to not have a bill of rights in the Constitution. These people became known as anti-Federalists.

The anti-Federalists did not believe Hamilton when he promised that the federal government would never threaten the freedoms owned by the people. The big fear was that a constitution by itself would not be enough to stop the government from turning into a power-mad dictatorship. They argued that a bill of rights would make it crystal clear to the people in charge of the government that government's powers had limits. The anti-Federalists wrote about this in essays of their own. The main purpose of the anti-Federalist essays was to convince people that the kind of constitution wanted by the Federalists had major problems. One was that it would leave the door open for the president to give himself so much power that he could easily be mistaken for a king or emperor.

Above: Founding Father Alexander Hamilton was against having a bill of rights. He believed that the U.S. Constitution all by itself was enough to guarantee people's rights.

A Duel to the Death

NEVER DISRESPECT Aaron Burr, under any circumstances. He might shoot you if you do. That's what happened to Alexander Hamilton in 1804. Hamilton disrespected Burr, so Burr killed him.

It was a fair fight, though. In fact, they shot it out in a duel. It was one of those old-fashioned kinds of duels where two men are each given a flintlock pistol, stand back to back, walk 10 paces, then turn and fire.

Burr, a former senator from New York, was vice president of the United States. Hamilton was a Founding Father who originally was a big opponent of the Bill of Rights. Burr challenged Hamilton to a duel after a newspaper published gossip about crude remarks supposedly made by Hamilton about Burr. During the duel, Hamilton fired first and missed. Burr fired back and hit Hamilton in the side. Hamilton died from the wound a day later, on July 12, 1804.

It was a double tragedy for Hamilton's wife. Their son Philip had died in a duel three years earlier using the exact same set of pistols. But it was also a tragedy for the country. Hamilton was a former secretary of the treasury and the founder of the first political party in the U.S., the Federalist Party.

Above: The duel between Alexander Hamilton and Aaron Burr.

Hamilton was born in 1755. He was a believer in natural law rights, but he didn't think ordinary people could be trusted to use their freedoms wisely. He wanted the United States to have a government similar to England's. But instead of a king, Hamilton thought the people should elect a president who would serve for life. He also thought each state's senators should serve for life.

Hamilton gave a big speech about his proposal when the Founding Fathers gathered in Philadelphia, Pennsylvania, in 1787 to create the Constitution. It was a terrific talk. Unfortunately for Hamilton, few took it seriously. Even so, Hamilton liked the Constitution that was produced at this convention. He worked very hard to get it approved by the legislature in his home state of New York. His state ratified the Constitution in 1788.

George Washington became the first president of the United States once the Constitution took effect. Washington chose Hamilton to be the nation's first secretary of the treasury in 1789. Hamilton accomplished many important things, including founding the United States Mint and the First Bank of the United States.

As the treasury secretary, Hamilton persuaded Congress to pass laws that gave the federal government more power than many of the Founding Fathers were comfortable with. Thomas Jefferson was one of those who disagreed with some of the things Hamilton had done. When Jefferson was elected president in 1801, he sought to roll back some of those laws.

SHOUTING MATCH

The Federalists and the anti-Federalists got into some very heated arguments. There was yelling and screaming. They threw things at each other. Occasionally, fists flew. In fact, it was hard to tell the difference between some of their meetings and an average modern school cafeteria lunch hour.

At the heart of these arguments was the question of whether the young United States even needed a constitution. The Constitution we have today did not exist when the United States was brand new. For about the first decade of its existence, the United States government operated under a set of rules called the Articles of Confederation. These rules put very little power in the hands of the federal government. Instead, most of the power was held by the individual states.

People such as Alexander Hamilton thought this system of confederation was completely upside down and illogical. They wanted the federal government to have the most power.

Right: A caricature of a fight between Federalist Roger Griswold and Republican Matthew Lyon in Congress, February 1789.

With such power, the federal government could properly protect the country against enemy attack, and prosperity could be spread far and wide. But the way the Confederation worked, only the states could collect taxes. That meant the federal government had to beg for money from each state if it needed to raise an army and a navy or build highways. Also, only the states could regulate commerce. As a result, each state had its own rules for how companies and shops were allowed to operate. Sometimes these rules made things that were perfectly legal for merchants to do in one state illegal to do in another. This made it harder for people to do business across state lines. Making business harder than it needed to be made it harder for prosperity to spread.

The Federalists began complaining loudly about these kinds of problems almost as soon as the Articles of Confederation took effect. In 1786, they at last convinced a number of states to schedule a huge meeting to talk about tossing out the Articles of Confederation. The meeting took place in Annapolis, Maryland. It went well enough that Congress agreed to schedule an even bigger meeting the next year in Philadelphia, Pennsylvania, to create the Constitution.

The Philadelphia meeting took place as promised. But the Constitution was not written in a single day. The meeting participants spent several months drafting the document before they were ready to send it to Congress. When Congress finally received it, there was much debate. Some liked it and some didn't. Those who didn't like it were upset that the Constitution did not include a bill of rights. When it came time to vote, Congress agreed to accept the Constitution without a bill of rights and to pass the new charter around to all the states for their approval.

Some of the biggest battles over the Constitution took place in the states. Some of the arguments were really nasty. For example, an important judge in Rhode Island who favored a bill of rights led a march of 1,000 men carrying guns, knives, clubs, and pitchforks into the state capital to stop the legislature from approving the Constitution. The judge was angry the Constitution did not include a bill of rights. The judge's message: sign it and you die.

The Rhode Island lawmakers managed to calm down the angry mob. Later, they did give their approval to the Constitution, but only after the document had already won ratification from the required number of other states.

Approving the Constitution was an especially explosive issue in Massachusetts. But it resulted in the way being paved for the Bill of Rights to be created. Anti-Federalists in the Massachusetts legislature used rare and little-known procedural tricks to bottle up efforts to approve the Constitution. They told the Federalists in the legislature that they would gladly stop using those tricks if the Federalists promised to demand of Congress the addition of a bill of rights to the Constitution.

The Federalists at first did not want to agree to any such thing. They told the anti-Federalists to go fly a kite. But the Federalists soon gave in when they saw that the anti-Federalists were not going to back down. The agreement worked out by the Federalists and anti-Federalists came to be called the famous Massachusetts Compromise.

Anti-Federalists in other states took note of what happened in Massachusetts.

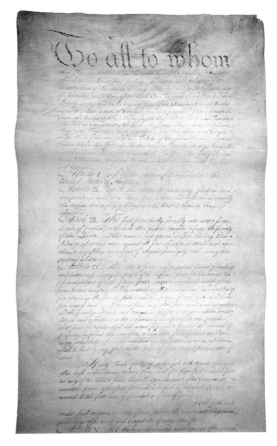

Above: A copy of the Articles of Confederation. This historical paper is housed in the National Archives building in Washington, D.C. The Articles of Confederation were adopted on November 15, 1777, in York, Pennsylvania, by the Second Continental Congress.

Then they too began using procedural tricks to give themselves bargaining power. The next five states to ratify the Constitution all did so by including a demand that Congress amend the Constitution with a bill of rights.

Those demands carried a lot of weight with Congress, which responded by authorizing a bill of rights for the Constitution. Congress then invited the states to send in suggestions for rights that should be chosen. More than 200 proposed amendments were eventually received.

HE KNEW SOMETHING EXCITING WAS HAPPENING

James Madison was the person who took the 200-plus suggested amendments from the states and then chose the best among them to be in the Bill of Rights. An interesting fact is that Madison was originally one of the biggest foes of a bill of rights in the Constitution. He was one of the essayists who helped Alexander Hamilton produce *The Federalist Papers*. Because of that, many people felt that Madison should not be allowed to work on the Bill of Rights. They wondered how he could possibly do a good job, considering how hard he had fought against any kind of bill of rights for the Constitution. They believed Congress should have given the job to someone who had been in favor of the Bill of Rights. But others thought Madison's war against the idea of a bill of rights would actually make him perfect for the job. The fact that he had been such a strong opponent practically guaranteed he wouldn't choose amendments that would handcuff the government and prevent it from protecting the country or promoting progress.

When Madison sat down at his desk to go through the more than 200 proposed amendments, he tried to keep in mind earlier bills of rights from other places that he thought were good models. One of these was the Magna Carta from England, which was written in the early 1200s. Another was England's 1689 Bill of Rights. Lastly and most importantly was the Virginia Declaration of Rights, which was written in 1776. The Virginia Declaration of Rights was perhaps the document Madison relied on most because it had been written just 20 or so years earlier and because it was based heavily on the theory of natural rights.

Above: Because Founding Father James Madison had originally argued against the Bill of Rights, people felt that he would choose only the best amendments to benefit the country.

MEET THE AUTHOR

Above: Many people call James Madison the "Father of the Bill of Rights." In 1809, he became the fourth president of the United States.

HE IS FAMOUS for writing the Bill of Rights, but it was his role as president of the United States for which James Madison is most celebrated. The biggest thing that happened during his presidency was the War of 1812. That was the war that gave America "The Star-Spangled Banner" as its national anthem.

The War of 1812 started after British sailors kept boarding unarmed American merchant ships and forcing the crews at gunpoint to join the British navy. The war did not go very well for the United States during most of the three years that it lasted. The lowest point came when the British army invaded and captured Washington, D.C. Madison and the entire government had to flee the city. As they glanced back over their shoulders, they could see the White House in flames.

The American forces fought as hard as they could. Eventually, they wore themselves out. However, the British were in no better shape. They too were exhausted. Finally, the two sides agreed they'd had enough fighting. They signed a peace agreement in 1815 called the Treaty of Ghent.

Neither England nor the United States had to give up any of their lands under the terms of the treaty. But the U.S. did gain two important things as a result of the war. First, no one ever again could question whether America had really won independence from England during the Revolutionary War. Until the end of the War of 1812, there had been doubters. Second, the War of 1812 jump-started America's change from a farm country to an industrial giant. During the war, the British navy cut off the United States from imported goods shipped across the Atlantic Ocean. American citizens responded by rushing to build factories so that the goods the young nation needed could be made in the U.S.A.

In addition to leading the nation during the War of 1812, James Madison is known for his role in bringing about the Louisiana Purchase. At the time, Madison was President Thomas Jefferson's secretary of state. The Louisiana Purchase brought the United States all of the lands held by France throughout the South and the Midwest. The United States nearly doubled in size the minute this deal was completed.

Madison was born in 1751. He lived to be 85 years old. Many people call him the "Father of the Constitution" because he did most of the work on the document. Some also called him the "Father of the Bill of Rights" for the same reason.

Madison was an impressive leader who knew how to make himself heard and win an argument. (Oddly, he was also a very shy man.) As a young adult, Madison came to believe America should have a strong federal government. Later, he changed his mind and decided the country would be better off if the federal government had only limited strength.

For a while, Madison was a leader of the Federalist Party. The Federalists wanted a strong federal government and were against having a bill of rights in the Constitution. Madison eventually left the Federalist Party to help Thomas Jefferson in 1791 start the Democratic-Republican Party. The purpose of this new party was to fight the Federalists, and they did a good job of it. By 1800, the Democratic-Republican Party was the leading political organization in the United States. However, the party fell to pieces in the 1820s. But one of those pieces regained its strength and went on to became the Democratic Party, which is one of the two main political parties today.

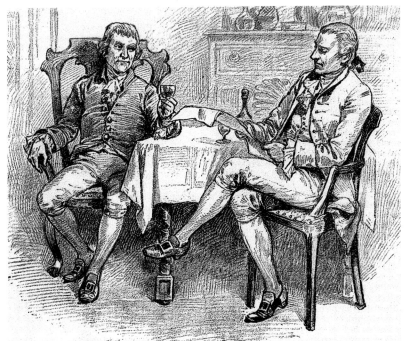

Left: James Madison sits with President Thomas Jefferson. As Jefferson's secretary of state, Madison helped bring about the Louisiana Purchase from France, doubling the size of the United States.

WHEN COPYING IS GOOD

THE BILL OF RIGHTS was created from copying, but not the bad kind of copying. James Madison, who wrote the Bill of Rights, didn't copy by looking over the shoulder of the Founding Father sitting in front of him. Instead, Madison used the good kind of copying. That's where you borrow somebody else's idea and make it better by adding fresh ideas of your own.

In the case of the Bill of Rights, Madison borrowed ideas from several sources. The most important of those sources was the Virginia Declaration of Rights. The Virginia

Declaration of Rights came from a Founding Father by the name of George Mason. Mason wrote the document in 1776 as part of the constitution of the state of Virginia. Virginia needed a constitution and a bill of rights because statehood was something brand new.

Left: Founding Father George Mason wrote most of the Virginia Declaration of Rights. It was adopted by the Virginia Constitutional Convention on June 12, 1776.

Mason and his fellow Virginians believed that rights did not come from kings or from governments. They believed in natural rights. They believed that a country is ruled by all the people together and that government is merely their servant.

These beliefs showed up everywhere in the Virginia Declaration of Rights. The charter included sections declaring freedom of the press, freedom of religion, a right to bear arms, freedom from unreasonable searches and seizures, a right to confront witnesses, a right to not self-incriminate, a right to a speedy trial, a right to a trial by jury, and freedom from cruel and unusual punishments.

Above: English landowners demanded some power over of their own destiny. Banding together, they forced King John to sign the Magna Carta in 1215.

Until 1776, Virginia was a colony of England. As a colony, it operated under the laws of England. One of the highest of those laws was the Act Declaring the Rights and Liberties of the Subject and Settling the Succession of the Crown.

That was a mouthful, so everyone called this law the English Bill of Rights. It was written in 1689. The idea of natural rights was still somewhat new in those times. But the people who wrote the English Bill of Rights liked the idea enough that they tried to weave some of it into the language of the law. Still, they had to be careful. The document they wrote had to please the king. Some of the freedoms the authors were able to include in the English Bill of Rights were: the right to bear arms as long as you were a member of the correct church, the right not to be thrown in prison or have all your property seized without first being given a trial, and the right not to be cruelly punished or harshly fined if found guilty of a crime.

George Mason used the English Bill of Rights as a starting point for his Virginia Declaration of Rights. So did James Madison in his work on the United States Bill of Rights. And everybody looked back to an even earlier document for freedom called the Magna Carta, which is Latin for "Great Charter." The Magna Carta was also from England, but it was written more than 450 years before the English Bill of Rights.

In the times leading up to the Magna Carta, the power of English kings was absolute. Laws were created by the king's decree, not by any kind of democratic process. In the year 1215, the biggest English landowners grew tired of their king's abuses of his power. So they banded together and seized control of London, the capital of England. They told the king they would give him back the city if he promised to sign a paper stating that he was transferring to them some of his powers. The powers taken from the king enabled the landowners to form a limited government and to ensure that people would no longer be imprisoned forever without first being given a trial. The king agreed to this. The paper he signed was the Magna Carta.

Above: The Magna Carta. This copy, from the year 1297, is on display in the National Archives building in Washington, D.C.

THE BILL OF RIGHTS IS APPROVED

The more James Madison worked on the Bill of Rights, the more excited he became. In fact, he was so enthusiastic that he ended up being the person who pushed Congress the hardest to adopt the Bill of Rights.

The version that Madison sent to Congress was slightly longer than what was finally approved. Madison's original version had 12 amendments. The first two were not ratified by the necessary three-fourths of the states, which is how the Bill of Rights came to be 10 amendments. One of the dropped amendments put a limit on how big the House of Representatives could become. The other one put a limit on how much money representatives and senators could give themselves as salary. However, this last one came back 200 years later and joined the United States Constitution as the Twenty-Seventh Amendment.

After Congress voted to accept the amendment proposals, it sent the Bill of Rights out to the states for ratification. As with the Constitution, the Bill of Rights attracted plenty of criticism. There was much heated debate in the state legislatures. By this time there were 14 states in the Union. That meant 11 states needed to approve the Bill of Rights in order for it to take effect. New Jersey was the first to vote yes. On December 15, 1791, Virginia became the 11th state to grant its approval, ushering in the Bill of Rights as an official part of the United States Constitution.

Above: James Madison's original version of the Bill of Rights had 12 amendments, but only 10 of those eventually made it into the finished document.

GLOSSARY

AMENDMENT

When it was created, the Constitution wasn't perfect. The Founding Fathers wisely added a special section. It allowed the Constitution to be changed by future generations. This makes the Constitution flexible. It is able to bend to the will of the people it governs. Changes to the Constitution are called amendments. The first 10 amendments are called the Bill of Rights. An amendment must be approved by two-thirds of both houses of Congress. Once that happens, the amendment must be approved by three-fourths of the states. Then it becomes law. This is a very difficult thing to do. The Framers of the Constitution didn't want it changed unless there was a good reason. There have been over 9,000 amendments proposed. Only 27 of them have been ratified, or made into law. Some amendments changed the way our government works. The Twelfth Amendment changed the way we elect our president. The Twenty-Second Amendment limits a president to two terms in office. Constitutional amendments have also increased the freedoms of our citizens. The Thirteenth Amendment finally got rid of slavery. And the Nineteenth Amendment gave women the right to vote.

BILL OF RIGHTS

The first 10 amendments to the United States Constitution make up what is known as the Bill of Rights. The Bill of Rights lists the special freedoms every human is born with and is able to enjoy in America. Also, the Bill of Rights tells the government that it cannot stop people from fully using and enjoying those freedoms unless the government has an extremely good reason for doing so.

CONSTITUTIONAL CONVENTION

The meeting of lawmakers who wrote the United States Constitution.

CONTINENTAL CONGRESS

The lawmakers who governed the 13 colonies after they declared their independence from Great Britain.

DICTATORSHIP

A country with a single leader who rules with total power. Citizens of a dictatorship have little or no say in how their country is run. Dictators usually gain their position, and keep their powers, through the use of military force. The Constitution was written to avoid dictatorships. It splits government into three distinct parts: the presidency, Congress, and the Supreme Court. This separation of power keeps any one individual from becoming a dictator.

FOUNDING FATHERS

The men who participated in the Constitutional Convention in 1787, especially the ones who signed the Constitution. Some of the Founding Fathers included George Washington, Benjamin Franklin, John Rutledge, Gouverneur Morris, Alexander Hamilton, and James Madison.

LEGISLATURE

A body of persons with the power to make, change, or repeal laws.

MILITIA

A group of citizens enrolled in military service during a time of emergency.

RATIFICATION

The process of making a proposed law or treaty officially valid. Constitutional amendments are ratified when they are approved by two-thirds of both houses of Congress, and by three-fourths of the states.

REVOLUTIONARY WAR

The war between Great Britain and its American colonies that lasted from 1775 to 1783. Also known as the War of Independence.

SUPREME COURT

The United States Supreme Court is the highest court in the country. There are nine judges on the Supreme Court. They make sure local, state, and federal governments are following the rules spelled out in the United States Constitution. Our understanding of the Constitution evolves over time. It is up to the Supreme Court to decide how the Constitution is applied to today's society. When the Supreme Court rules on a case, other courts in the country must follow the decision in similar situations. In this way, the laws of the Constitution are applied equally to all Americans.

WARRANTS

A legal document issued by a government official authorizing a police search of a specific building or area. A warrant may also be issued for a person's arrest or for some other action in regards to seeking justice.

INDEX